Evangelism
an
Social R

An Evang

Published on behalf of
The Lausanne Committee for World Evangelization
and the World Evangelical Fellowship by
THE PATERNOSTER PRESS
EXETER

This edition published by
The Paternoster Press Ltd, Exeter, UK

First impression 1982

EVANGELISM AND SOCIAL RESPONSIBILITY
An Evangelical Commitment

This Report, *Evangelism and Social Responsibility*, was written during the international Consultation on the Relationship between Evangelism and Social Responsibility, held at Grand Rapids, Michigan, June 19-25, 1982. It was drafted by members of the Consultation, the Drafting Committee being under the chairmanship of the Rev. John Stott, who was also responsible for the final editing. The Consultation was sponsored by the Lausanne Committee for World Evangelization and the World Evangelical Fellowship. In arranging for the publication of this Report and encouraging the study of it, neither the Lausanne Committee for World Evangelization nor the World Evangelical Fellowship necessarily endorses every opinion expressed in it.

AUSTRALIA:
Bookhouse Australia Ltd.,
P.O. Box 115,
Flemington Markets, NSW 2129

SOUTH AFRICA:
Oxford University Press,
P.O. Box 1141, Cape Town

British Library Cataloguing in Publication Data

Evangelism and social responsibility.
1. Evangelistic work 2. Church and the world
269'.2 BV3790

ISBN 0-85364-364-4

Typeset by Photoprint, Paignton, Devon
Printed and bound in Great Britain
at The Pitman Press, Bath

Contents

FOREWORD 5

INTRODUCTION 9
(a) The Context of the Consultation
(b) Scripture and Culture

1 A CALL TO WORSHIP AND THANKSGIVING 12

2 A CALL TO WORLD EVANGELIZATION 13
(a) Contemporary Need
(b) A Definition
(c) Motivation for Evangelism

3 A CALL TO SOCIAL RESPONSIBILITY 16
(a) Contemporary Need
(b) A Definition
(c) Motivation for Social Responsibility

4 THE RELATIONSHIP BETWEEN EVANGELISM AND SOCIAL RESPONSIBILITY 19
(a) Historical Background
(b) Particular Situations and Gifts
(c) Three Kinds of Relationship
(d) The Question of Primacy
(e) Some Examples

5 THE GOOD NEWS OF THE KINGDOM 28
(a) Salvation
(b) The Kingdom of God
(c) The Signs of the Kingdom
(d) The Extent of the Kingdom

6 HISTORY AND ESCHATOLOGY 36
(a) False Dreams
(b) Differing Millenarian Views
(c) Judgment to Come
(d) The Eschatological Vision
(e) Continuity
(f) The Christian Hope

7 GUIDELINES FOR ACTION 43
(a) Forms of Evangelism and Social Responsibility
1. Social Service and Evangelism
2. Social Action and Evangelism
(b) Agents of Evangelism and Social Responsibility
1. Evangelism and Social Service
2. Evangelism and Social Action
(c) The Local Church in a Free Society
1. Intercession
2. Love
3. Teaching
4. Power
5. Vocations
6. Groups
7. Resources
(d) The Church under Repression
1. Consistency
2. Love
3. Witness
4. Solidarity
5. Suffering

CONCLUSION: A CALL TO OBEDIENCE 62

APPENDIX A: MEMBERS OF THE CONSULTATION 63

APPENDIX B: THE PAPERS AND THEIR WRITERS 64

Foreword

Evangelicals and evangelism have always been bracketed. So much so that the adjectives 'evangelical' and 'evangelistic' have often been identified in the popular mind. It is not at all surprising, therefore, that whenever evangelicals have become concerned about social issues, some eyebrows have been raised, and questions have been asked whether the cause of the gospel is not about to be betrayed.

The history of the ecumenical movement has unfortunately strengthened evangelical suspicions of social involvement. Modern ecumenism was born in the missionary enthusiasm — even euphoria — of the 1910 World Missionary Conference in Edinburgh. John Mott its chairman described as a 'longstanding reproach' to the church the fact that there were still millions of people who had never heard of Christ. The church must develop a strategic plan, he urged, 'for the evangelization of the whole of this multitude'. From this high point of commitment to world evangelism, however, there seems to have been a steady decline. The convening by evangelicals of the two Congresses on World Evangelization at Berlin in 1966 and at Lausanne in 1974 must unfortunately be understood, at least in part, as a loss of confidence in the World Council of Churches. But then leaders of the World Council have also been justly critical of many of us evangelicals for our lack of social concern.

This polarisation became particularly visible in 1980 when the conference *Your Kingdom Come* (sponsored by the WCC's Commission on World Mission and Evangelism) was held in Melbourne in May, and the following month the consultation *How Shall They Hear*? (sponsored by the Lausanne Committee) took place at Pattaya, Thailand. Neither group had intended that these meetings should be juxtaposed in this way, although perhaps it served to highlight the continuing tension. A number of evangelicals attended both conferences and found reasons for hope in both. For a perusal of the documents makes it plain that there was much common ground between them. Nevertheless, the emphasis was different. At Melbourne the necessity of proclamation was clearly recognized, but the cries of the poor, the hungry and the oppressed predominated. At Pattaya also the cries of the needy were heard (one mini-consultation focused on refugees, and another on the urban poor), but the call to proclaim the gospel to the unevangelized predominated.

This, then, was the historical run-up to the Consultation on the Relationship between Evangelism and Social Responsibility held at Grand Rapids in June 1982. The planning group took great pains to ensure a balanced representation among participants between geographical regions, denominational backgrounds and evangelical viewpoints. It also defined clearly the goals of the Consultation. It expressed its resolve to study 'Scripture, history, theology and the contemporary church, and the interaction among them', and its hope and prayer for God's blessing in the following ways:

'1. that we shall come to understand each other better and to appreciate each other's points of view more fully.
2. that we shall reach a greater unity of mind on the relationship between evangelism and social responsibility, not by a superficial semantic consensus but by a real theological agreement according to Scripture.
3. that we shall commit ourselves, and encourage other believers to commit themselves, to a yet more active fulfilment of our evangelistic and social responsibilities.'

In spite of these declared goals, I confess that I arrived in Grand Rapids with a considerable degree of apprehension. The papers and responses, circulated in advance, had not only been critical of each other's positions but even in some cases sharply so. How then could we possibly expect to reach accord? Yet underneath our natural fears there was a confidence that God could unite us, if we humbled ourselves under the authority of his Word. And so it proved. For me it was another and dramatic demonstration of the value of international conferences. When we remain apart from one another, and our only contact with one another is the lobbing of hand grenades across a demilitarized zone, our attitudes inevitably harden and our mental images of each other become stereotyped. But when we meet face to face (or, as our American friends vividly express it, 'eyeball to eyeball'), and listen not only to each other's arguments but to the cherished convictions which lie behind the arguments, then we develop towards one another a new understanding, respect and love. This is not to say that we agree about everything (as our Report makes plain), but that our agreements are far greater than our residual differences.

The group entrusted with the task of drafting the Report consisted of Gottfried Osei-Mensah from Africa and Bong Rin Ro from Asia (co-chairmen of the Consultation), David Wells (USA), Samuel Olson (Latin America) and myself (Europe). Early drafts were approved by the group, and then submitted to plenary sessions throughout the Friday and the Saturday morning of the Consultation. The revised draft, incorporating a large number of requested amendments, was re-submitted to participants by mail. A very few minor adjustments have subsequently been made to the text.

As we look back on our Grand Rapids experience, we are profoundly grateful to God for the common mind and heart which he gave us. We commend our Report to the study of individual Christians and of local churches. And we pray that our verbal commitment to the evangelistic and social responsibilities which God has laid upon us will express itself in increasingly practical and dedicated action.

John R. W. Stott
Chairman, Drafting Committee

Introduction

(a) The Context of the Consultation

Jesus Christ calls all his followers to witness to him in word and deed, that is, to share his good news with others and to serve them according to their needs.

In the Lausanne Covenant, which was adopted at the end of the International Congress on World Evangelization in 1974, Paragraph 4 is entitled "The Nature of Evangelism" and Paragraph 5 "Christian Social Responsibility". But the Covenant leaves these two duties side by side without spelling out their relationship to each other, except to say in Paragraph 6 that "in the church's mission of sacrificial service, evangelism is primary".

As the years have passed, it has become increasingly necessary to complete Lausanne's unfinished business and to define more clearly what is included in "social responsibility", whose responsibility it is, and how it relates to evangelism. For many fear that the more we evangelicals are committed to the one, the less we shall be committed to the other; that if we commit ourselves to both, one is bound to suffer; and in particular that a preoccupation with social responsibility will be sure to blunt our evangelistic zeal.

So, in the conviction that evangelical Christians, who seek to live under the lordship of Christ and the authority of Scripture, and who pray to be guided by the Holy Spirit, should not be divided on an issue of such importance, it was decided to call an international consultation to study the matter. Jointly sponsored by the Lausanne Committee for World Evangelization and the World Evangelical Fellowship, the Consultation would focus on Scripture, church history, modern theologies and the contemporary church, in order to help participants understand each other better, reach a greater unity of mind, and commit themselves to a yet more active fulfilment of their evangelistic and social responsibilities.

We have not been disappointed. Fifty evangelical leaders from 27 different countries have spent a week together at Grand Rapids, Michigan. Each day began with Bible study and prayer. Eight papers, and the responses to them, have been presented to us. The issues raised by them we have discussed in both small groups and plenary sessions, and we have been encouraged by case studies from several different cultures. Throughout the week, through patient listening to one another, we have grown in mutual understanding and respect. Although our agreement is not total, it is substantial, and we have been given grace to face our disagreements with charity.

This statement is a summary of the consensus which has emerged, but it makes no attempt to conceal our differences. Although participants have not been asked to endorse it individually, they thoroughly scrutinized its first draft and amended it. We now publish it with the desire to share with others the fruits of our discussion and in the hope that they will be stimulated, as we have been, to more conscientious evangelism and social responsibility.

(b) Scripture and Culture

The stated goals of the Consultation indicated that we would focus first and foremost on Holy Scripture. We have been determined, therefore, to let our minds be formed not by any human ideology but by the Word of God.

We have found it a struggle, however. For all of us are to some extent conditioned by the cultural environment in which we live, by our ideological settings and theological traditions, and this tends to determine what we are able to "see" in Scripture. It is not that God's Word is unclear in itself, nor that its meaning is captive to any culture. The problem lies rather within our minds as we read. The assumptions we bring with us, which are often insufficiently examined and corrected in the light of God's Word, distort our understanding of it. "Now we see in a mirror dimly" (I Cor. 13:12).

How else can we explain some of the painful anomalies that soon came to light in our discussion? To give a few examples: we heard of some Christians in a Confucian culture who, because of its assumption of the ultimate harmony of all things, have surrendered their belief in the uniqueness of Christ as Saviour. Under the pressure of religious pluralism, others have fallen into universalism. In some parts of the United States there are churches which still close their doors to blacks, and remain oblivious to the indignities to which discrimination has brought them, while at the same time proclaiming the love of God. In South Africa, social policy and legislation are built on the theory of the inviolable diversity of the races. Many churches, whose members are sincere Christian people, nevertheless share this view of racial irreconcilability, while continuing to preach the good news of reconciliation. In Europe and North America, secularism — which is a child of the Enlightenment — has even invaded the lives of Christians and effectively banished the reality of God from much of what they do.

It is easy to censure fellow believers in distant parts, however, and to occupy ourselves with removing splinters from their eyes while failing to perceive the logs in our own. It has become apparent during our Consultation that those of us who live in affluence do not feel the pain and humiliation of poverty as readily as do those who live among the poor. To the former, social responsibility may remain a topic for academic debate; to the latter, it is a self-evident Christian obligation. Yet moral blindspots are not peculiar to white or black, affluent or poor, north or south. They are a symptom of that fall in which we have all participated. It is our sin, as it comes to expression in our various cultural assumptions and tries to find justification in them, which often blinds our eyes to what God wants us to see in his Word. An acknowledgement of this tragic fact at the beginning of our Consultation challenged us to listen all the more attentively to one another and to God's Word.

1 A Call to Worship and Thanksgiving

God created and redeemed our world in order to reveal his infinite majesty and his eternal love. Therefore, the primary sin is to refuse to honour him as God or to give him thanks (Rom. 1:21), while the supreme duty of his redeemed people is to worship him in humble praise and obedience. "We love, because he first loved us" (I John 4:19).

From this adoring and loving encounter with God, there immediately flows a desire to share his love with our fellow human beings, both by telling them how God in Christ has loved them and by serving them in deeds of mercy and justice.

Only if they are rooted in a vertical relationship to God in worship can the church's two ministries of *kerygma* (proclamation) and *diakonia* (service) be held in proper balance and tension. Only in this way, too, can evangelism and social responsibility be kept from degenerating into merely human activity and even propaganda. The mission of any church can fall into this trap.

It is therefore urgent to heed the pre-eminent call to worship and thanksgiving.

2 A Call to World Evangelization

(a) Contemporary Need

When we met at Lausanne in 1974, we calculated that more than 2,700 million people were still unevangelized. Now, eight years later, we believe that the number has risen to three billion, and that this comprises many thousands of people groups. We cannot think of them as statistics, however. They are human beings like ourselves. Yet, though created by God like God and for God, they are now living without God. The tragedy of this is painful, and the task of overcoming it is enormous. It calls for concerted prayer and evangelism on an unprecedented scale.

(b) A Definition

But what is evangelism? This is the definition given in the Lausanne Covenant (Paragraph 4):

> To evangelize is to spread the good news that Jesus Christ died for our sins and was raised from the dead according to the Scriptures, and that as the reigning Lord he now offers the forgiveness of sins and the liberating gift of the Spirit to all who repent and believe. Our Christian presence in the world is indispensable to evangelism, and so is that kind of dialogue whose purpose is to listen sensitively in order to understand. But evangelism itself is the proclamation of the historical, biblical Christ as Saviour and Lord, with a view to persuading people to come to him personally and so be reconciled to God. In issuing the gospel invitation we have no liberty to conceal the cost of discipleship. Jesus still calls all who would follow him to deny themselves, take up their cross, and identify themselves with his new community. The results of evangelism include obedience to Christ, incorporation into his church and responsible service in the world.

We heartily endorse this statement, and we wish to emphasize that reconciliation to God lies at the very heart of the good news. Our only criticism is that the statement sounds somewhat impersonal, since neither the evangelist nor the evangelized is characterized in it as a person of flesh and blood. Yet that is what they both are, and evangelism involves a personal encounter between them. The most essential qualities of gospel messengers are loyalty to the biblical gospel and personal authenticity. They must embody the good news they proclaim. Few things repel people more than hypocrisy, and few things attract them more than integrity.

As for the persons who hear the Gospel, we acknowledge the need to approach them with great sensitivity. Many will already have been convicted of their sin and guilt, and it will be possible at once to share with them the good news of forgiveness. Others will be oppressed by a different sense of alienation. So we shall have to begin where they are, with their "felt needs", and then lead them to where they have to come, that is, to Christ as Saviour from their deepest need — their sinful separation from God.

(c) Motivation for Evangelism

There are many incentives to evangelism. To begin with, there is simple obedience to the Great Commission, and to the Lord of the Great Commission, to whom all authority has been given (Matt. 28:18-20). Then there is the terrible knowledge we have that human beings without Christ are lost or "perishing" (e.g., John 3:16; I Cor. 1:18), and our earnest desire in love to reach them with the Gospel before it is too late. Another powerful motive is zeal or "jealousy" for the glory of Christ, whom God has super-exalted in order that every knee should bow to him and every tongue confess him Lord (Phil. 2:9-11).

Yet we believe that the most basic of all motives lies in the very nature of God himself, and in his saving work by which he revealed himself. We do not exaggerate when we affirm that the living God is a missionary God. He created all humankind, is "the God of the spirits of all flesh", and when calling Abraham promised through his posterity to bless "all the families of the earth".

Next, Jesus Christ during his public ministry sent his disciples to "the lost sheep of the house of Israel", and subsequently he commissioned them to go and make disciples of all the nations. Between these two missions lay his death and resurrection. He died on the cross for the sins of the world, and was raised and exalted to be Lord. The church's universal mission derives from Christ's universal authority.

Thirdly, the Holy Spirit is a missionary Spirit, and Pentecost was a missionary event. He gave his people power for witness, as Jesus promised, and thrust them out to the ends of the earth, as Jesus foretold (Acts 1:8).

This Trinitarian basis for mission is primary. It is the missionary heart of God himself, Father, Son and Holy Spirit. If he yearns in his love for his lost world, we his people must share his yearning. Commitment to world mission is unavoidable, and indifference to it inexcusable.

3 A Call to Social Responsibility

(a) Contemporary Need

We are appalled to know that about 800 million people, or one-fifth of the human race, are destitute, lacking the basic necessities for survival, and that thousands of them die of starvation every day. Many more millions are without adequate shelter and clothing, without clean water and health care, without opportunities for education and employment, and are condemned to eke out a miserable existence without the possibility of self-improvement for themselves or their families. They can only be described as "oppressed" by the gross economic inequality from which they suffer and the diverse economic systems which cause and perpetuate it.

The oppression of others is political. They are denied fundamental human rights by totalitarian regimes of the extreme left or right, while if they protest they are imprisoned without trial, tortured, and killed. Yet others suffer discrimination on account of their race or sex. And all of us are oppressed by global problems which seem to defy solution — conditions of overpopulation and famine, the exploitation of non-renewable resources of energy, the spoliation of the environment, community violence, war, and the ever-present threat of a nuclear holocaust.

All these are rooted in the profound sinfulness of humankind, and they demand from the people of God a radical response of compassion. Only the Gospel can change human hearts, and no influence makes people more human than the Gospel does. Yet we cannot stop with verbal proclamation. In addition to worldwide evangelization, the people of God should become deeply involved in relief, aid, development and the quest for justice and peace.

(b) A Definition

Here is the paragraph on "Christian Social Responsibility" in the Lausanne Covenant (Paragraph 5):

> We affirm that God is both the Creator and the Judge of all men. We therefore should share his concern for justice and reconciliation throughout human society and for the liberation of men from every kind of oppression. Because mankind is made in the image of God, every person, regardless of race, religion, colour, culture, class, sex or age, has an intrinsic dignity because of which he should be respected and served, not exploited. Here too we express penitence both for our neglect and for having sometimes regarded evangelism and social concern as mutually exclusive. Although reconciliation with man is not reconciliation with God, nor is social action evangelism, nor is political liberation salvation, nevertheless we affirm that evangelism and socio-political involvement are both part of our Christian duty. For both are necessary expressions of our doctrines of God and man, our love for our neighbour and our obedience to Jesus Christ. The message of salvation implies also a message of judgment upon every form of alienation, oppression and discrimination, and we should not be afraid to denounce evil and injustice wherever they exist. When people receive Christ they are born again into his kingdom and must seek not only to exhibit but also to spread its righteousness in the midst of an unrighteous world. The salvation we claim should be transforming us in the totality of our personal and social responsibilities. Faith without works is dead.

(c) Motivation for Social Responsibility

Again, as in evangelism so in social responsibility, we discern the fundamental basis for our actions in the character of God himself. He is the God of justice, who in every human community hates evil and loves righteousness. He is also the God of mercy. In the first Bible study of our Consultation we read of him that, though he made the universe, he nevertheless humbles himself to care for the needy, "executes justice for the oppressed", and "gives food to the hungry". In addition, "the Lord sets the prisoners free; the Lord opens the eyes of the blind. The Lord lifts up those who are bowed down; the

Lord loves the righteous. The Lord watches over the sojourners, he upholds the widow and the fatherless; but the way of the wicked he brings to ruin'' (Psalm 146:5-9). We recognize that we have neither the authority nor the power to do everything God does. Nevertheless, since this text shows us the kind of God he is, and since these concerns of his were further expressed in the demands of his law and prophets, it is indisputable what kind of people we should be, seeking justice, freedom and dignity for all, especially the powerless who cannot seek it for themselves.

It is no surprise that Jesus reflected this lovingkindness of God his Father. He had compassion on the hungry, the sick, the bereaved, the outcast. He had compassion on the crowds because they were harassed and helpless, like sheep without a shepherd. And always his compassion issued in appropriate action.

Moreover, the first fruit of the Holy Spirit is love (Gal. 5:22). It is therefore he who gives his people a tender social conscience, and impels them to immerse themselves in humanitarian relief, development, and the search for justice.

Thus we find that there is a Trinitarian basis for our social duties, just as there is for our evangelistic outreach. We who claim to belong to God and who worship him as Father, Son and Holy Spirit, must express our worship in these activities. *Orare est laborare.*

4 The Relationship between Evangelism and Social Responsibility

(a) Historical Background

It appears to us that evangelism and social concern have been intimately related to one another throughout the history of the church, although the relationship has been expressed in a variety of ways. Christian people have often engaged in both activities quite unselfconsciously, without feeling any need to define what they were doing or why. So the problem of their relationship, which led to the convening of this Consultation, is comparatively new, and for historical reasons is of particular importance to evangelical Christians.

The Great Awakening in North America, the Pietistic Movement in Germany, and the Evangelical Revival under the Wesleys in Britain, which all took place in the early part of the 18th century, proved a great stimulus to philanthropy as well as evangelism. The next generation of British evangelicals founded missionary societies and gave conspicuous service in public life, notably Wilberforce in the abolition of the slave trade and of slavery itself, and Shaftesbury in the improvement of conditions in the factories.

But at the end of the 19th century and the beginning of the 20th, the so-called "social gospel" was developed by theological liberals. Some of them confused the Kingdom of God with Christian civilization in general, and with social democracy in particular, and they went on to imagine that by their social programmes they could build God's Kingdom on earth. It seems to have been in over-reaction to this grave distortion of the Gospel that many evangelicals became suspicious of social involvement. And now that evangelicals are recovering a social conscience and rediscovering our evangelical social heritage, it is understandable that some of our brothers and sisters are looking askance at us and suspecting us of relapsing into the old heresy of the social gospel. But the responsible social action which the biblical Gospel lays upon us, and the liberal "social gospel" which was a perversion of the true Gospel, are two quite different things. As we said in the Lausanne Covenant, "we . . . reject as a proud self-confident dream the notion that man can ever build a utopia on earth" (Paragraph 15).

Another cause of the divorce of evangelism and social responsibility is the dichotomy which has often developed in our thinking. We tend to set over against one another in an unhealthy way soul and body, the individual and society, redemption and creation, grace and nature, heaven and earth, justification and justice, faith and works. The Bible certainly distinguishes between these, but it also relates them to each other, and it instructs us to hold each pair in a dynamic and creative tension. It is as wrong to disengage them, as in "dualism", as it is to confuse them, as in "monism". It was for this reason that the Lausanne Covenant, speaking of evangelism and socio-political involvement, affirmed that they "are both part of our Christian duty" (Paragraph 5).

(b) Particular Situations and Gifts

In wanting to affirm that evangelism and social responsibility belong to each other, we are not meaning that neither can ever exist in independence of the other. The Good Samaritan, for example, if we may characterize him as a Christian, could not have been blamed for tending the wounds of the brigands' victim and failing to preach to him. Nor is Philip to be blamed for preaching the Gospel to the Ethiopian eunuch in his chariot and failing to enquire into his social needs. There are still occasions when it is legitimate to concentrate on one or the other of these two Christian duties. It is not wrong to hold an evangelistic crusade without an accompanying programme of social service. Nor is it wrong to feed the hungry in a time of famine without first preaching to them, for, to quote an African proverb, "an empty belly has no ears". It was similar in the days of Moses. He brought the Israelites in Egypt the good news of their liberation, "but they did not listen to him, because of their broken spirit and their cruel bondage" (Exod. 6:9).

There is another justification for sometimes separating evangelism and social action, in addition to the existential demands of a particular situation: namely, the distribution of spiritual gifts. The church is a charismatic community, the Body of Christ, whose members are endowed by the Holy Spirit with different gifts for different forms of ministry. Some are gifted to be "evangelists" (Eph. 4:11), while others are called to "service" (Rom. 12:7; I Pet. 4:11) or to "acts of mercy" (Rom. 12:8). Whatever our gifts may be, we are neither to depreciate them nor to boast of them (I Cor. 12:14-26), but rather to use them for the common good.

The best example of the outworking of this principle occurs in Acts 6 where the apostles, who had been called to "prayer and the ministry of the Word", were in danger of becoming preoccupied with "serving tables", that is, with caring for the material needs of the church's widows. So seven men were appointed to perform this social service, although Stephen and Philip also did some preaching (Acts 6:8-15; 8:5-13). This left the apostles free to concentrate on the pastoral ministry for which they had been commissioned, although they also retained a social concern (e.g., Gal. 2:10). Still today, Christ calls some to pastoral, others to social, others to evangelistic ministries; in fact, there is a wide diversity of spiritual gifts, callings and ministries within the Body of Christ.

(c) Three Kinds of Relationship

Having seen that both particular situations and specialist callings can legitimately separate our evangelistic and social responsibilities, we are now ready to consider how in general they relate to one another. What has emerged from our discussion is that there is no one relationship in which they are joined, but that there are at least three equally valid relationships.

First, social activity is a *consequence* of evangelism. That is, evangelism is the means by which God brings people to new birth, and their new life manifests itself in the service of others.

Paul wrote that "faith works through love" (Gal. 5:6), James that "I will show you my faith by my works" (James 2:18), and John that God's love within us will overflow in serving our needy brothers and sisters (I John 3:16-18). As Robert E. Speer wrote about the Gospel in 1900: "wherever it goes, it plants in the hearts of men forces that produce new lives; it plants in communities of men forces that create new social combinations." We have heard of evangelists in our own day who, during their missions or crusades, actively encourage Christians (including new converts) to become involved in programmes to meet specific local, human needs. This effectively highlights the serving dimension of Christian conversion and commitment.

We can go further than this, however. Social responsibility is more than the consequence of evangelism; it is also one of its principal aims. For Christ gave himself for us not only "to redeem us from all iniquity" but also "to purify for himself a people of his own who are zealous for good deeds" (Tit. 2:14). Similarly, through the Gospel we are "created in Christ Jesus for good works which God prepared beforehand, that we should walk in them" (Eph. 2:10). Good works cannot save, but they are an indispensable evidence of salvation (James 2:14-26).

In saying this, we are not claiming that compassionate service is an automatic consequence of evangelism or of conversion, however. Social responsibility, like evangelism, should therefore be included in the teaching ministry of the church. For we have to confess the inconsistencies in our own lives and the dismal record of evangelical failure, often as a result of the cultural blindspots to which we have already referred. This has grave consequences. When we do not allow the Word of God to transform us in all areas of our personal and social life, we seem to validate the Marxist criticism of religion.

Secondly, social activity can be a *bridge* to evangelism. It can break down prejudice and suspicion, open closed doors, and gain a hearing for the Gospel. Jesus himself sometimes performed works of mercy before proclaiming the Good News of the Kingdom. In more recent times, we were reminded, the construction of dams by the Basel missionaries in Northern

Ghana opened a way for the Gospel, and much missionary medical, agricultural, nutritional and educational work has had a similar effect. To add a contemporary western example, a recent crusade in an American city was preceded and accompanied by a "Love in Action" programme, with the evangelist's encouragement. Several "social uplift" groups co-operated and were able to extend their ministries to the inner city poor. As a result, we were told, a number of people came under the sound of the Gospel who would not otherwise have come to the crusade.

Further, by seeking to serve people, it is possible to move from their "felt needs" to their deeper need concerning their relationship with God. Whereas, as another participant put it, "if we turn a blind eye to the suffering, the social oppression, the alienation and loneliness of people, let us not be surprised if they turn a deaf ear to our message of eternal salvation." We are aware of the danger of making "rice Christians", that is, of securing converts only because of the physical benefits we offer. But we have to take this risk, so long as we retain our own integrity and serve people out of genuine love and not with an ulterior motive. Then our actions will be "not bribes but bridges — bridges of love to the world."

Thirdly, social activity not only follows evangelism as its consequence and aim, and precedes it as its bridge, but also accompanies it as its *partner*. They are like the two blades of a pair of scissors or the two wings of a bird. This partnership is clearly seen in the public ministry of Jesus, who not only preached the Gospel but fed the hungry and healed the sick. In his ministry, *kerygma* (proclamation) and *diakonia* (service) went hand in hand. His words explained his works, and his works dramatized his words. Both were expressions of his compassion for people, and both should be of ours. Both also issue from the lordship of Jesus, for he sends us out into the world both to preach and to serve. If we proclaim the good news of God's love, we must manifest his love in caring for the needy. Indeed, so close is this link between proclaiming and serving, that they actually overlap.

This is not to say that they should be identified with each other, for evangelism is not social responsibility, nor is social responsibility evangelism. Yet, each involves the other.

To proclaim Jesus as Lord and Saviour (evangelism) has social implications, since it summons people to repent of social as well as personal sins, and to live a new life of righteousness and peace in the new society which challenges the old.

To give food to the hungry (social responsibility) has evangelistic implications, since good works of love, if done in the name of Christ, are a demonstration and commendation of the Gospel.

It has been said, therefore, that evangelism, even when it does not have a primarily social intention, nevertheless has a social dimension, while social responsibility, even when it does not have a primarily evangelistic intention, nevertheless has an evangelistic dimension.

Thus, evangelism and social responsibility, while distinct from one another, are integrally related in our proclamation of and obedience to the Gospel. The partnership is, in reality, a marriage.

(d) The Question of Primacy

This brings us to the question whether the partnership between evangelism and social responsibility is equal or unequal, that is, whether they are of identical importance or whether one takes precedence over the other. The Lausanne Covenant affirms that "in the church's mission of sacrificial service evangelism is primary" (Paragraph 6). Although some of us have felt uncomfortable about this phrase, lest by it we should be breaking the partnership, yet we are able to endorse and explain it in two ways, in addition to the particular situations and callings already mentioned.

First, evangelism has a certain priority. We are not referring to an invariable *temporal* priority, because in some situations a social ministry will take precedence, but to a *logical* one. The very fact of Christian social responsibility presupposes socially responsible Christians, and it can only be by evangelism and discipling that they have become such. If social activity is a consequence and aim of evangelism (as we have asserted), then evangelism must precede it. In addition, social progress is being hindered in some countries by the prevailing religious culture; only evangelism can change this.

Secondly, evangelism relates to people's eternal destiny, and in bringing them Good News of salvation, Christians are doing what nobody else can do. Seldom if ever should we have to choose between satisfying physical hunger and spiritual hunger, or between healing bodies and saving souls, since an authentic love for our neighbour will lead us to serve him or her as a whole person. Nevertheless, if we must choose, then we have to say that the supreme and ultimate need of all humankind is the saving grace of Jesus Christ, and that therefore a person's eternal, spiritual salvation is of greater importance than his or her temporal and material well-being (cf. II Cor. 4:16-18). As the Thailand Statement expressed it, "of all the tragic needs of human beings none is greater than their alienation from their Creator and the terrible reality of eternal death for those who refuse to repent and believe." Yet this fact must not make us indifferent to the degradations of human poverty and oppression. The choice, we believe, is largely conceptual. In practice, as in the public ministry of Jesus, the two are inseparable, at least in open societies. Rather than competing with each other, they mutually support and strengthen each other in an upward spiral of increased concern for both.

(e) Some Examples

The three relationships between evangelism and social responsibility need not occur in isolation from each other. Instead, they often blend together in such a way that it is difficult to distinguish them. This was made clear to us as we listened to a number of case studies.

The "Precious Jewels Development" project in Cebu City, Philippines, is a many-pronged effort by Christians to serve their neighbours, improving their means of local livelihood, offering education and child care, developing a nutritional programme, and giving emergency relief. In one respect, it is simply an expression of love, the natural consequence of the knowledge of Christ which the Gospel has brought. In another, it has been a bridge to evangelism. Non-Christians "opened themselves" to Christians. Their reserve was melted, and they became ready to hear the Gospel. Thus, social service, evangelism's consequence and bridge, also became its partner. God himself was loving them, one of them said, through the preaching of the Gospel and the meeting of their practical needs.

Another project in the Philippines ("Project Gamtabeng") has come to the aid of a hill tribe whose very existence was threatened by urbanization and industrialization. Medical, agricultural and educational development have gone hand in hand with evangelism and church planting. A convert summed up the Project's aims by saying "Through Project Gamtabeng, I became an heir to my Father's heaven and earth."

We also heard about some nomadic Maasai people of Northern Kenya who had come to Christ. Amidst dancing and singing, they were being welcomed into the church by the Anglican bishop. As they celebrated, however, he noticed that half of them were either blind or nearly so. "This convinced me," he said, "that we cannot evangelize the spiritually blind and leave them in their physical blindness." Immediately, therefore, a health care programme was developed.

Next, we were told of an Indian couple, both doctors, who have laboured for more than 20 years in Jamkhed, Maharashtra. They trained despised outcaste widows in the elements of pre- and post-natal care, proved their credentials as healers by establishing a small operating theatre, and taught out of the Gospels how Jesus gave dignity to women. As a result, child mortality has been reduced almost to zero, social justice has increased and fear has diminished, and many people in seventeen villages, which for 50 years had not responded to the Good News, are now turning to Jesus.

In addition, we learned about the Voice of Calvary ministries in Mississippi, where for 22 years the Gospel has been shared, and the physical, spiritual, economic, social and material needs of people have been met. Evangelism, community development and racial reconciliation through the church have gone hand in hand. The reason for this holistic ministry is that its pioneer came face to face with the cycle of poverty in which the people were trapped. They were so preoccupied with the struggle to survive, that they could not attend to spiritual realities. It would have been almost impossible to offer Jesus Christ to them and ignore their other needs. So the Gospel of love is verbalized and actualized simultaneously.

5 The Good News of the Kingdom

Having suggested three ways in which evangelism and social responsibility are related to one another, we come to an even more basic way in which they are united, namely by the Gospel. For the Gospel is the root, of which both evangelism and social responsibility are the fruits. As Good News of God's love in Christ, the Gospel demands both to be preached and to be lived. Once we have come to know it, we are obliged to share it with others and to "adorn" it by good deeds (Tit. 2:10).

So what is the Good News? No simple answer can be given, since a variety of models is developed in the New Testament. At this Consultation, however, we have concentrated on two comprehensive models. We have thought of the Gospel both as "good news of salvation" (Eph. 1:13) and as "good news of the Kingdom of God" (Matt. 4:23; Mark 1:14,15; Luke 4:43).

(a) Salvation

We are all agreed that salvation is a broad term, in the sense that it embraces the totality of God's redemptive purpose.

It begins with *new life*. Through the substitutionary death and historical resurrection of Jesus, the individual believer is "ransomed, healed, restored, forgiven". Saved from guilt and the judgment of God, he or she is adopted into God's family as his child.

Salvation continues with the *new community*. For salvation in the Bible is never a purely individualistic concept. As in the Old Testament, so in the New, God is calling out a people for himself and binding it to himself by a solemn covenant. The members of this new society, reconciled through Christ to God and one another, are being drawn from all races and cultures. Indeed, this single new humanity — which Christ has created and in which no barriers are tolerated — is an essential part of the Good News (Eph. 2:11-22).

Thirdly, salvation includes the *new world* which God will one day make. We are looking forward not only to the redemption and resurrection of our bodies, but to the renovation of the entire created order, which will be liberated from decay, pain and death (Rom. 8:18-25). Of this cosmic renewal the resurrection of Christ was the beginning and the pledge.

Having agreed on these three dimensions of salvation (personal, social and cosmic), we went on to pose a further question: is salvation experienced only by those who consciously confess Christ as Lord and Saviour? Or is it right in addition to refer to the emergence of justice and peace in the wider community as "salvation", and to attribute to the grace of Christ every beneficial social transformation? Some of us do not find salvation-language inappropriate for such situations, even when Christ is not acknowledged in them. Most of us, however, consider that it is more prudent and biblical to reserve the vocabulary of salvation for the experience of reconciliation with God through Christ and its direct consequences. None of us would dream of following those who have portrayed Hitler's Germany or Mao's China or Castro's Cuba as having experienced "salvation", though all of us are united in wishing to honour Christ as universal Lord.

(b) The Kingdom of God

It is well known that Jesus came preaching the Kingdom of God. According to the Synoptic Gospels, the Kingdom was the major theme of his sermons and parables. Although "the Kingdom of God" is largely replaced by "eternal life" in John's Gospel and by the lordship of Christ in Paul's letters, so that we recognize the diversity of salvation models and wish to avoid committing ourselves exclusively to any one of them, nevertheless the Kingdom is a richly suggestive concept, with significant applications to the modern world. Hence our decision to focus on it.

The Kingdom of God is the rule of God, and the whole Bible declares that God is King. As the Creator, he is both King of nature (sustaining what he has made) and King of history (ordering the life of nations). "The Lord reigns" is a frequent shout of joy in the Old Testament, expressing Israel's confidence in the providential rule of God over the world. Over themselves Israel knew that Yahweh reigned in a special way. For even after the people had demanded a king like other nations, Israel did not cease to be a theocracy. Yet her kings were only a poor approximation to Yahweh's ideal of kingship. So he began to promise through his prophets that one day he would send his own king, anointed with his Spirit, to reign in righteousness and peace over all peoples and for ever.

"The time has come," Jesus announced as he began his public ministry, "the Kingdom of God is near. Repent and believe the Good News" (Mark 1:15). Thus Jesus brought the Kingdom with him. "Eschatology invaded history." "The person of Jesus and the presence of God's Kingdom are inseparably connected." Only those enter it who humble themselves like a little child and are born again.

The Kingdom of God is both a present reality and a future expectation. As a present reality, now that Jesus' physical presence has been withdrawn from the earth, his Holy Spirit establishes it in the lives of his people. For the King must never be thought of apart from his subjects, the messianic community, over which he rules. Moreover, his rule takes the form of both total blessing (salvation, in fact) and total demand (obedience and service).

Christians have often debated the relationship between the church and the Kingdom. We must not identify them, but neither must we separate them. The church is the community in which God's kingly rule is revealed, which therefore witnesses to the divine rule, and is the firstfruits of the redeemed humanity (James 1:18). It lives by new values and standards, and its relationships have been transformed by love. Yet it continues to fail. For it lives in an uneasy tension between the "already" and the "not yet", between the present reality and the future expectation of the Kingdom.

(c) The Signs of the Kingdom

Evangelism is the proclamation of this Kingdom in the fulness of its blessings and promise, which are also called "salvation". Moreover, Jesus did more than preach the Kingdom; he demonstrated its reality with "signs of the Kingdom", public evidence that the Kingdom he was talking about had come. We believe that signs should validate our evangelism, too, and we have spent time discussing what they should be.

Since "the reason the Son of God appeared was to destroy the devil's work" (I John 3:8), he inevitably came into collision with the prince of darkness. The signs of the Kingdom were evidences that the devil was retreating before the advance of the King. As Jesus put it, once the strong man has been overpowered by the Stronger One, his possessions can be taken from him (Matt. 12:29; Luke 11:22).

The signs reflect this. We list them in approximately the order in which they appeared, although this is not necessarily an order of importance.

The *first* sign of the Kingdom was (and still is) Jesus himself in the midst of his people (Lk. 17:21; Matt. 18:20), whose presence brings joy, peace, and a sense of celebration (John 15:11; 16:33; Mk. 2:18-20).

The *second* is the preaching of the Gospel. There was no Gospel of the Kingdom to proclaim until Christ arrived. Now that he has come, however, the Good News of the Kingdom must be preached to all, especially to the poor (Lk. 4:18,19; 7:22). The preaching of the Kingdom points people to the Kingdom itself.

The *third* sign of the Kingdom was exorcism. We refuse to demythologize the teaching of Jesus and his apostles about demons. Although the "principalities and powers" may have a reference to demonic ideologies and structures, we believe that they certainly are evil, personal intelligences under the command of the devil. Demon possession is a real and terrible condition. Deliverance is possible only in a power encounter in which the name of Jesus is invoked and prevails.

The *fourth* sign of the Kingdom was the healing and the nature miracles — making the blind see, the deaf hear, the lame walk, the sick whole, raising the dead (Lk. 7:22), stilling the storm, and multiplying loaves and fishes. We all agree that these were not only signs pointing to the reality of the Kingdom's arrival, but also anticipations of the final Kingdom from which all disease, hunger, disorder and death will be for ever banished. We also agree that God is still free and powerful, and performs miracles today, especially in frontier situations where the Kingdom is advancing into enemy-held territory. Some of us think we should expect miracles as commonly as in the ministry of Jesus and his apostles (e.g., John 14:12), while others draw attention to the texts which describe these miracles as authenticating their unique ministry (e.g., Heb. 2:3,4; II Cor. 12:12).

A *fifth* sign of the Kingdom is the miracle of conversion and the new birth. Whenever people "turn to God from idols, to serve the living and true God" (I Thess. 1:9,10), a power encounter has taken place in which the spell of idols, whether traditional or modern, and of the spirits, has been broken. God's power for salvation is displayed in the Gospel (Rom. 1:16), and converts who have been rescued from darkness to light and from the power of Satan to God (Acts 26:18) are said to have "tasted . . . the powers of the age to come" (Heb. 6:5).

A *sixth* sign of the Kingdom is the people of the Kingdom, in whom is manifested that cluster of Christlike qualities which Paul called "the fruit of the Spirit". For the gift of the Spirit is the supreme blessing of the Kingdom of God. Where he rules, love, joy, peace and righteousness rule with him (Gal. 5:22,23; Rom. 14:17). Moreover, love issues in good works. Thus, if the Gospel is Good News of the Kingdom, good works are the signs of the Kingdom. Good News and good works, evangelism and social responsibility, are once again seen to be indissolubly united.

The *seventh* sign of the Kingdom, we suggest, is suffering. It was necessary for the King to suffer in order to enter into his glory. Indeed, he suffered for us, leaving us an example that we should follow in his steps (I Pet. 2:21). To suffer for the sake of righteousness or for our testimony to Jesus, and to bear such suffering courageously, is a clear sign to all beholders that we have received God's salvation or Kingdom (Phil. 1:28,29; cf. II Thess. 1:5).

(d) The Extent of the Kingdom

If these are the signs of the Kingdom, manifesting its present reality and pointing forward to its final consummation, how extensive is the Kingdom they signify?

In one sense, as we have seen, God's rule extends only over those who acknowledge it, who have bowed their knee to Jesus and confessed his lordship (Phil. 2:9-11). These God "has delivered . . . from the dominion of darkness and transferred to the Kingdom of his beloved Son" (Col. 1:13). Apart from them, the whole world is "in the power of the evil one", its "ruler" and "god" (I John 5:19; John 12:31; II Cor. 4:4), for "we do not yet see everything in subjection to" Jesus (Heb. 2:8; cf. Ps. 110:1; Acts 2:35).

Yet in another sense, the Risen Lord claimed that "all authority in heaven and on earth" had been given to him (Matt. 28:18). For already God has "put all things under his feet and has made him head over all things for the church" (Eph. 1:22). His titles are "King of kings and Lord of lords" and "the ruler of princes on earth" (Rev. 1:5; 19:16).

How can these two perspectives be fused? How can Christ claim universal authority if the whole world still lies in Satan's power? The answer is that over his redeemed people Jesus is King *de facto*, while it is only *de jure* that he is presently King over the world, his right being still challenged by the usurper. Perhaps, therefore, we should reserve the expression "the Kingdom of God" for the acknowledged rule of Christ, since this is the new thing he inaugurated at his coming, while referring to the more general "sovereignty" of God over all things.

It is important to maintain the tension between what Christ rules *de facto* and *de jure*. For if we assume that all authority has in fact been given to him, we shall not take seriously the evil powers which have not yet capitulated. If, on the other hand, our horizon is bounded by the community in which the King is consciously confessed, we may be tempted to dismiss the rest of the world as beyond redemption. From these extremes of naive optimism and dark pessimism we return to the radical realism of the Bible, which recognizes both the defeat of evil and its refusal to concede defeat. This double conviction will persuade us to work hard in evangelism and in the quest for justice, while at the same time putting our whole trust and confidence in God.

During the interim period between the two comings of Christ, between his victory over evil and evil's final capitulation and destruction, what should be the relations between the Kingdom community and the world?

First, the new community should constitute a challenge to the old. Its values and ideals, its moral standards and relationships, its sacrificial life-style, its love, joy and peace — these are the signs of the Kingdom, as we have seen, and present the world with a radically alternative society. All our words of love and deeds of love must express our wholehearted submission to the Lord of love himself.

Secondly, as the world lives alongside the Kingdom community, some of the values of the Kingdom spill over into society as a whole, so that its industry, commerce, legislation and institutions become to some degree imbued with Kingdom values. So-called "Kingdomized" or "Christianized" society is not the Kingdom of God, but it owes a debt to the Kingdom which often is unrecognized.

The "overspill" model has its limitations, however, because it pictures the two communities as independent of one another, like two vessels standing side by side, the contents of one spilling over into the other. The salt, light and yeast metaphors which Jesus employed are more dynamic, since each implies the penetration of the old community by the new. The light shines into the darkness, the salt soaks into the meat, the yeast causes fermentation in the dough. So Jesus intends his followers neither to withdraw from the world in order to preserve their holiness, nor to lose their holiness by conforming to the world, but simultaneously to permeate the world and to retain their Kingdom distinctives. Only so can they share the Good News with credibility. Only so can they be effective agents for cultural, social and political change. Indeed, as "the Lord blessed the Egyptian's house for Joseph's sake" (Gen. 39:5), so we believe he blesses the world through the ministry of, and for the sake of, his redeemed people.

Meanwhile, we do not forget that God is directly at work in

his world, apart from the agency of his people. In his common grace he continues without intermission to sustain the earth and its creatures, to grant life and health, to give sunshine and rain, to maintain the cycle of the seasons, to cause the ground to be fruitful, to preserve society from disintegration, and to give to all humankind (who bear his image and have his law written in their hearts — Rom. 2:14,15) a certain appreciation of justice, freedom, beauty, dignity and peace.

While we gladly recognize these works of God in the world, both directly and through his people, they are not what Jesus meant by his Kingdom. It is, therefore, our urgent responsibility to summon all people in Christ's name to turn and humble themselves like little children, as we have sought to humble ourselves, in order to enter the Kingdom and receive its priceless blessing, the salvation of God (Matt. 18:3).

6 History and Eschatology

We devoted a whole day of our Consultation to "history and eschatology", that is, to the relationship between *on the one hand* what we do now in the historical process and what God is doing since the last days began when the Kingdom was inaugurated, and *on the other* what God is going to do on the Last Day when he ushers in the fulness of the Kingdom.

(a) False Dreams

We saw our study as being all the more important because we human beings are inveterate dreamers. We cannot live only for today; we must have some hope for tomorrow which will sustain us in our pilgrimage. Consequently, like the pseudo-prophets of the Old Testament, we have a constant tendency to fabricate false dreams, visions which come out of our own minds, and not from the Lord (cf. Jer. 23:25-32).

We have been conscious of the special need to distinguish the social responsibility to which we as Christians are called, its reasons and its content, from that which modern ideologies have generated. Both dogmatic and Messianic Marxisms, for example, proclaim a bogus millennium which recognizes neither the Creator of the world, nor his Christ. Yet they anticipate that by changing social structures, frequently by violent means, they will by human effort alone bring about a fully just and perfect society. A programme for change such as this, because it denies the stubborn reality of evil and ignores our deepest human needs, is bound to end in failure, even in disaster.

We also reject the Messianic Western dream which aims at erecting a counterfeit materialistic Kingdom. We recognize, of course, the divine command to subdue the earth and harness its resources for the good of all. But selfish secular materialism pursues its own economic growth irrespective of the need to conserve the environment and to serve the development of the poorer nations. It is characterized by self-absorbed individualism and insensitive affluence, which are incompatible with Christian — let alone truly human — values, and which unwittingly foster increasing inequality between the rich and the poor.

Again, we cannot join those who call for a new political world order, based on a new world religion concocted from a synthesis of all religions, as the only means of escaping from the threats of global calamity. We, too, recognize with sober realism the terrible potential for destruction in human life. But we are convinced that only the power of God manifest in the forgiveness and recreative power of Christ can restore to us that order, meaning, freedom, dignity and responsibility which the world so desperately needs.

It was, therefore, with relief that we turned from all ideological substitutes to the authentic Christian hope, to the vision of the triumphant return of Jesus, and of the Kingdom he will consummate, which God has revealed to us in his Word. Our concern was to relate this hope to history, and to our concrete duties within history. In particular, we asked ourselves whether there is any connection between our eschatological outlook and the attitude we adopt towards evangelism and social responsibility. We are conscious that more biblical study and historical research are needed before we will be ready to handle this question with greater confidence. For the present, we feel able to contribute only tentatively to the debate.

(b) Differing Millenarian Views

To begin with, we thought about the millennium and about its influence on Christian behaviour at different periods of church history. We tried to discern whether there is any correlation between the three traditional varieties of millennialism and the vigour with which social responsibility and evangelism have been pursued in the history of the church. Without doubt, our understanding of the millennium affects the way in which we view the world. The degree of hope which we sustain seems to be proportionate to the degree to which we see the Kingdom of God as an already present reality or as a largely future expectation.

Since all three views of the millennium were represented at our Consultation, and since we desired to give one another liberty on this matter and not to convert one another to our own position, we moved on from our millenarian differences to seek a common eschatological motivation for evangelism and social responsibility. Of course, Christians are given in the New Testament many other reasons and motives for good living and good works, which we did not consider. The following eschatological incentives were put forward.

(c) Judgment to Come

The first was judgment. A great deal of teaching by Jesus and his apostles linked present responsibility with future judgment. Jesus told us to be alert, sober and busy in his service, because we do not know when our Lord will come. But we do know that when he comes he will call us to account (e.g., Mk. 13:33-36; Lk. 12:35-40; Matt. 25:14-30).

The conscientious dedication of the apostle Paul to evangelism seems to have been related directly to his sense of accountability. "Knowing the fear of the Lord," he wrote, "we persuade men." "Men-persuading" is a clear reference to his evangelistic methods, as we know from the Acts, and "the fear of the Lord" to appearing before Christ's judgment seat, of which he has written in the previous verse (II Cor. 5:10,11).

The same motivation can sustain us in our works of philanthropy, as is evident from the sheep and the goats passage which we studied together one morning. In this solemn description of the day of judgment, the "sheep" or the "righteous", who are "blessed" and welcomed into the Kingdom, are those who have ministered to Christ in the hungry and thirsty, the naked and sick, the strangers and the prisoners. The "goats", on the other hand, who are "cursed" and dismissed to eternal punishment, are those who have failed to minister to Christ in the needy. Whether Christ's "brethren" are his followers in general, as other passages seem to indicate (e.g. Matt. 12:46-50; Heb. 2:10-18), or in particular his messengers, as may be suggested by the "cup of cold water" passage (Matt. 10:9-15,40-42), or may include the rest of needy humankind with whom Christ humbly identifies himself, the principal message is the same. As the rest of the New Testament teaches, the dead will be judged "by what they have done" (e.g. Rev. 20:13), and our deeds will include either the loving service of those in need or a scandalous indifference to their plight. These will be an acid test whether we are true believers, or unbelievers.

Neither of these two passages of Scripture can possibly mean that we can gain entry to heaven by our good works. To interpret them in this way would be to turn the Gospel upside down. What they are emphasizing is that though we are justified by grace alone through faith alone, we shall be judged by those good works of love through which our secret faith is made public.

(d) The Eschatological Vision

We are united in rejecting utopic visions, which are dreams of human accomplishment. The eschatological vision is totally different, however, because it is a revelation of what God himself is going to do in the end. This vision can give both direction and inspiration to our present duty. We do not, of course, presume to imagine that we can do now what God will do then. Nor will every part of our life on earth have a counterpart in the final state (e.g., there will be no marriage after the Resurrection — Mk. 12:25).

Nevertheless, the glimpses God has given us of the end disclose the kind of community life which is pleasing to him. Twice Peter tells us "what sort of persons" we ought to be in this life on account of what is going to happen at the end. He likens the coming destruction of the present evil order to the flood, except that it will be by fire instead of water, and urges us in consequence to "lives of holiness and godliness". Then he passes from the destruction of the old order to the creation of the new. He argues that because in the new heavens and the new earth "righteousness dwells", therefore we must be zealous to be found by Christ "without spot or blemish, and at peace". In other words, because righteousness and peace will be characteristics of the eternal kingdom, we need to pursue them in the Kingdom's present manifestation (II Pet. 3:1-14).

We believe that, in a similar way, the vision of the countless multitude before God's throne, redeemed from every nation (Rev. 7:9), who will constitute the final fulfilment of God's promise to give Abraham a countless posterity (Gen. 12:1-3), should be a powerful incentive to us to obey the Great Commission, to go and make disciples of all nations, and to seek to make our churches a foretaste of the heterogeneous heavenly community.

If that aspect of the eschatological vision is a stimulus to evangelism, others should prove a stimulus to social responsibility. If in heaven they will "hunger no more, neither thirst any more" (Rev. 7:16), should we not feed the hungry today? And if in the end "they shall beat their swords into ploughshares, and their spears into pruning hooks, neither shall they learn war any more" (Micah 4:3; Is. 2:4), does that not mean that war is incompatible with the perfect will of God? Not that the state can now discard its responsibility to enforce justice and order (Rom. 13:1-4), any more than we can expect lambs and lions to lie down together now. But does not the promise of final peace tell us that, even if (as some Christians have always believed) war may be in some circumstances the lesser of two evils, we should all nevertheless seek to be peacemakers?

In these ways the eschatological vision can direct and motivate our Christian action, while at the same time we must never forget the fallenness of this world or the wickedness of the principalities and powers.

(e) Continuity

The words "continuity" and "discontinuity" have kept recurring throughout our Consultation. That is to say, will the final Kingdom enjoy some continuity with its present manifestation, or will the future be discontinuous with the present, so that nothing will survive the judgment except those who by God's sheer grace are the heirs of his Kingdom?

We have not been able to reach complete agreement on this matter. Some of us, vividly aware of the evil of this present age and of the glory that is to be revealed, emphasize the destructive nature of God's judgment and the newness of his new creation. Others of us believe that, just as after the new birth we are not a different person but the same person remade, so the universe is going to experience a new birth (*palingenesia*, Matt. 19:28). That is, God is going to re-create it, and not create another universe *ex nihilo*. Indeed, Paul likens the pains of the created order to the birthpangs of the new (Rom. 8:18-25; cf. Mk. 13:8).

We all believe this about our bodies, for the principle of continuity is evident in the resurrected body of Jesus. Although, as Paul expresses it, our new body will be as different from the old as a flower differs from its seed, nevertheless there will be a continuity between the two (I Cor. 15:35-46). And later he grounds his argument for sexual self-control and a right use of our bodies not only on what they are (members of Christ and temples of the Holy Spirit) but on what they are going to be: "The body is not meant for immorality, but for the Lord, and the Lord for the body. And God raised the Lord and will also raise us up by his power" (I Cor. 6:12-20). On this double resurrection, of the Lord Jesus and of our bodies, the apostle bases his plea for purity.

We are on more uncertain ground, however, when we ask how many of our present works will be carried over into eternity. Certainly evangelism has eternal consequences, since converts receive God's free gift of eternal life. So does our teaching, if we build with "gold, silver and precious stones" upon the foundation of Christ (I Cor. 3:10-15). But what about our social activity? We are told of those who "die in the Lord" that "their deeds follow them" (Rev. 14:13; cf. I Cor. 13:13). We also are told that the kings of the earth will "bring their glory" into the New Jerusalem, and that they will "bring into it the glory and the honour of the nations", while what will be excluded is everything "unclean" (Rev. 21:24-27). This has seemed to many to teach that whatever is beautiful, true and good in human cultures, once purged of everything which defiles, will be consummated in the final Kingdom. Those who have the assurance of this continuity find in it a strong incentive to social and cultural involvement.

(f) The Christian Hope

In whatever more precise ways we may formulate these motivations of judgment, vision and continuity, we all are agreed that our Christian hope focuses on the personal, visible and glorious return of our Lord Jesus Christ, on the resurrection from death, and on the perfected Kingdom which his appearing will bring. Also, we all are agreed that we are to live our lives and do our works in the conscious expectation of his coming. This confidence will make us committed to world evangelization (Matt. 24:14), "zealous for good deeds" (Tit. 2:13,14), faithful to one another in the fellowship (Heb. 10:25), and courageous in suffering (II Tim. 4:6-8; Rev. 2:25). With great firmness we therefore reject what has been called "eschatological paralysis". On the contrary, before the Lord comes, and in preparation for his coming, we are determined to get into the action. This is to "live anticipatorily", to experience the power, enjoy the community and manifest the righteousness of the Kingdom *now,* before it is consummated in glory.

7 Guidelines for Action

Much of our debate has been at a theological level, for we have felt the need to wrestle with the issues which relate to salvation and Kingdom, history and eschatology. Nevertheless, all our theologizing has been with a view to determining what practical action we should take to forward the mission which God has given us. In particular, we have considered in what forms our evangelistic and social concerns should be expressed, what agencies should undertake the work, and how different political and cultural situations will affect it.

(a) Forms of Evangelism and Social Responsibility

We have all been familiar for years with different forms of evangelism (personal evangelism, local church evangelism, mass evangelism, cross-cultural evangelism, etc.). But we have been less clear about the different forms in which our social concern should be manifested. Throughout our Consultation we have spoken of "social responsibility", "social ministries", "social assistance", "social service", "social action", "social justice", and (as in the Lausanne Covenant) "socio-political activity". We believe that a failure to define these terms has contributed to the continuing suspicion which surrounds every Christian activity described as "social". It may be easiest to divide our Christian social responsibility into two kinds, which for simplicity's sake we will call "social service" and "social action", and which can be distinguished from each other in several ways:

Social service	*Social action*
Relieving human need	Removing the causes of human need

Philanthropic activity	Political and economic activity
Seeking to minister to individuals and families	Seeking to transform the structures of society
Works of mercy	The quest for justice

In making this necessary functional distinction, we recognize that in practice it is not as neat as it looks. On the one hand, social action of a political kind lacks integrity if it is not supported by a personal commitment to social service. On the other, some works of mercy have inescapably political implications — for example, teaching the oppressed to read and write, visiting a banned person in South Africa, or sending food to Poland or North Vietnam.

1. Social Service and Evangelism

The first of these two kinds of social ministry is universally accepted as a Christian obligation; there is nothing controversial about it. Just as we are called to personal evangelism, so we are called to personal service. Jesus, we are told, both "went about . . . preaching and bringing the good news", and "went about doing good" (Luke 8:1; Acts 10:38).

All Christians should follow his example — although, to be sure, our way of sharing the Good News may not be only by preaching. Both personal evangelism and personal service are expressions of compassion. Both are forms of witness to Jesus Christ. And both should be sensitive responses to human need. The evangelist seeks to discover the principal point of felt need — for example, a sense of guilt or shame or fear, moral failure, personal loneliness, a lack of self-worth or significance, domestic unhappiness, a hunger for transcendence, lack of education, social repression, or demon activity. Similarly, a person's social needs may range from the physical (food, clothing, shelter or health care), through the psychological (anxiety, alienation, emotional unbalance) to the economic (poverty, illiteracy, unemployment). We will come to political needs later. Even in welfare states there are always areas of human need which government and voluntary agencies do not fully cover, and which Christians can take the initiative to meet.

"Development" could be put into a separate category, but it probably should be bracketed with philanthropic service, even though some community development projects embrace a whole village, town or district. It is very welcome that many welfare agencies have expanded their emphasis in recent years from aid to development, and many medical missions from curative medicine to community health. To help people learn to help themselves not only makes better sense economically, but it is also more conducive to human dignity. It is important, therefore, to ensure that self-help programmes genuinely enable people to stand on their own feet and are not devious paternalistic ploys to reinforce dependence, even subservience.

If Christian people are to get involved in humanitarian work, whether in the form of helping a neighbour or of sharing in an aid or development project, considerable sacrifices in time, energy and money will be needed. Authentic personal evangelism is equally costly. We see Christ's call to service, both evangelistic and social, as an important challenge to our self-centred, self-loving "me generation".

2. *Social Action and Evangelism*

The other kind of social responsibility is the quest for justice. It looks beyond persons to structures, beyond the rehabilitation of prison inmates to the reform of the prison system, beyond improving factory conditions to securing a more participatory role for the workers, beyond caring for the poor to improving — and when necessary transforming — the economic system (whatever it may be) and the political system (again, whatever it may be), until it facilitates their liberation from poverty and oppression. Such social changes often necessitate political action (for politics is about power), and some evangelicals fear it because they imagine it will entail civil strife and even revolution. But this is not what we mean by "socio-political involvement". We are thinking rather of political processes which are consistent with biblical principles — such as the rights of the individual and of minorities, respect for civil authority, the welfare of the whole community, and justice for the oppressed.

The Bible lays great emphasis on both justice (or righteousness) and peace. For God is the author of both, and both are essential characteristics of his Kingdom. We, therefore, who claim to be members of his Kingdom, must not only seek justice for others but must "do justice" ourselves (Mic. 6:8), in relation to our family, our fellow workers, and any servants or employees we may have. In the same way, it is not enough to "seek peace and pursue it"; we must also ourselves, so far as it depends on us, "live peaceably with all" (I Pet. 3:11; Rom. 12:18). This applies to churches as well as individual Christians. If discrimination and disunity are tolerated in the church, how can we denounce them in the nation? Conversely, it is churches which visibly demonstrate the righteousness and peace of the Kingdom which will make the greatest evangelistic and social impact on the world. The salt must retain its saltness, Jesus said; otherwise, it is good for nothing (Matt. 5:13).

(b) Agents of Evangelism and Social Responsibility

One of the points of tension emerging during the Consultation has concerned the allocation of responsibilities. Granted that evangelism and social service/action are Christian responsibilities, who is responsible for what? What should be undertaken by individual Christians, what by groups, and in particular what is to be the role of the church as church?

1. Evangelism and Social Service

We all agree that alongside personal evangelism there should be personal social service. Individual Christians should be involved in both, according to their opportunities, gifts and callings.

The parallel is similar in the local church. Just as each local church has an inescapable responsibility before God to bring the Gospel to all the people who reside and work in its neighbourhood, so the social needs of the neighbourhood should be a special concern of the local church.

There is also an important place for both church groups and para-church groups. We shall have more to say about the former when we come to our section on "The Local Church in a Free Society". Para-church organizations, both for evangelism and for social responsibility, have an indispensable part to play in Christian outreach, especially if they specialize in kinds of ministry which no church can manage on its own, and provided that they accept a measure of responsibility to the churches.

2. Evangelism and Social Action

What about social action of a political kind, in distinction to social service of a philanthropic kind? Does social action belong to the mission of the church as church, or is it the prerogative of individual believers who make up the church, and of groups?

We have no doubt about individuals and groups. The church should encourage its members to become conscientious citizens, to take the initiative to found and operate social programmes, to inform themselves about political issues, and to advocate or dissent according to their conscience.

Since individual action is usually limited in its effects, however, Christians should also be encouraged to form or join groups and movements which concern themselves with specific needs in society, undertake research into social issues, and organize appropriate action. We welcome the existence and activity of such groups, for they supplement the church's work in many important areas. Christians should also be encouraged to participate responsibly in the political party of their choice, their labour union(s) or business association(s), and similar movements. Whenever possible, they should form a Christian group within them, and/or start or join a Christian party, union or movement, in order to develop specifically Christian policies.

From the activity of individuals and groups, we come back to the church. Should the church get involved in politics, or keep out? Some argue that churches which engage in socio-political action, especially on controversial issues, lose members and missionaries, because the action stirs up controversy. Others counter that different factors like theological liberalism and loss of confidence in the Gospel are the real cause of dwindling numbers.

This issue is not only pragmatic, however; it is essentially theological. Behind the debate lie our differing ecclesiologies and, in particular, our differing understandings of the relationship between church and state, between the Kingdom of God and what has been called the "Kingdom of Caesar". At least three traditions on Christian political involvement, all deriving from the European Protestant Reformation, have been represented in our Consultation. All agree that the Kingdom of God is distinct from the political realm. One sees the Kingdom as *opposed* to that realm, and pleads for a Christian community witness independent of political institutions. A second tradition sees the Kingdom as *separate* from the political realm, though parallel to it, and urges that Christians participate in that realm, though as citizens (not as church members) guided by Christian moral principles. The third tradition sees the Kingdom of God as penetrating and *transforming* the political realm; it argues that political involvement belongs to the witness not only of Christian individuals and groups but also of churches.

This discussion is far from being irrelevant to evangelism. People's hearts are often opened to the Gospel when they see that we genuinely care for them as persons rather than merely as souls. When they perceive that the Gospel is about the mercy and justice of God which were reconciled at Christ's cross, and see his mercy and justice still active in the situation today, they are likely to be the more ready to come to Christ.

(c) The Local Church in a Free Society

In spite of our differing theological and cultural backgrounds, on account of which some of us assign social action (of a political kind) to individuals and groups rather than to churches, all of us agree that the church has definite evangelistic and social responsibilities. This applies especially to the local church, which should be committed to the total well-being of the community in which it is permanently situated. Some of these duties belong to all churches, others only to churches in a free or open society. We shall have more to say in the next section about the particular case of churches under repression.

1. Intercession

"First of all," wrote Paul to Timothy, "I urge that supplications, prayers, intercessions, and thanksgivings be made for all men, for kings and all who are in high positions, that we may lead a quiet and peaceable life, godly and respectful in every way. This is good, and it is acceptable in the sight of God our Saviour, who desires all men to be saved and to come to the knowledge of the truth'' (I Tim. 2:1-4). Thus does the apostle give priority to prayer among the church's public duties, in particular prayer for the civil authorities, and he goes on to link it to both peace and salvation.

We are convinced that the living God hears and answers the prayers of his people, that by prayer we can enter into the unseen spiritual conflict and bind Satan in the name of Christ, and that there is special power in corporate prayer when ''two of you (or more) agree on earth about anything you ask'' (Matt. 18:19). Yet we are ashamed that our practice falls far short of our principle. Often the pastoral prayer in public worship is brief and perfunctory; the petitions are so unimaginative and stale as to border on ''vain repetitions''; and the people doze and dream instead of praying.

We resolve ourselves, and call upon our churches, to take much more seriously the period of intercession in public worship; to think in terms of 10 or 15 minutes rather than five; to invite lay people to share in leading, since they often have deep insight into the world's needs; and to focus our prayers both on the evangelization of the world (closed lands, resistant peoples, missionaries, national churches, etc.) and on the quest for peace and justice in the world (places of tension and conflict, deliverance from the nuclear horror, rulers and governments, the poor and needy, etc.). We long to see every Christian congregation bowing down in humble and expectant faith before our Sovereign Lord.

2. Love

If evangelism and social responsibility are twins, their mother is love. For evangelism means words of love and social service/action means deeds of love, and both should be the natural overflow of a community of love. We do not think the local church can reach out to its neighbourhood with any degree of credibility unless and until it is filled with the love of God.

This love will manifest itself first in the *philadelphia*

("brotherly love") which binds Christian brothers and sisters together. Such a loving fellowship has great evangelistic power. For it is only when we love one another, as Christ has loved us, that everybody will know we are his disciples (John 13:34,35). Further, the invisible God who once made himself visible in Christ now makes himself visible in us, if we love one another: "Nobody has ever seen God; but if we love one another, God abides in us and his love is perfected in us" (I John 4:12).

But the love of God cannot possibly be bottled up within the Christian community; it breaks out in compassion for the world. It yearns for the salvation of sinners, so that Christ's lost sheep may be gathered safely into his flock. It yearns also to alleviate the material needs of the poor, the hungry and the oppressed, so that if we close our hearts against the needy, we cannot claim that God's love abides in us (I John 3:17). Love for God and love for neighbour belong inextricably together, as Jesus taught (Mk. 12:28-34; cf. I John 4:19-21).

We are convinced that the Christian impact on society (both evangelistic and social) depends even more on quality than on numbers, and that the distinctive quality of Christians is love.

3. *Teaching*

Every Christian congregation, of course, should be preaching and teaching the Gospel, year in year out, in season and out of season, with biblical faithfulness, contemporary relevance and urgent boldness. We believe the church languishes whenever the Word of God is neglected, and flourishes whenever it is honoured. We desire to call our churches back to biblical preaching for both evangelism and edification.

But we have to teach our people the law as well as the Gospel, that is, obedience as well as forgiveness, the moral demands of the Kingdom as well as its gift of salvation. Indeed, it is the calling of preachers, like Paul in Ephesus, "not to shrink from declaring" to the people "anything that is profitable", indeed "not to shrink from declaring to them the whole counsel of God" (Acts 20:20,27). This will include rebuking evil in all its ugly manifestations.

Thorough teaching of the Word of God is even more important in our day, in which many Christians are bewildered by contemporary problems. They read about them in the newspaper and hear about them on radio or television; shall such topics then be excluded from the pulpit? We are not now referring to issues which are controversial even among Christians (we will come to these in the next paragraph), but to fundamental modern challenges to the teaching of the Bible. People need help to resist the pressures of secular thought and to take a firm stand on the moral principles of Scripture. So we must help them to discern the moral issues in each question, to understand them and to hold them fast. In addition, they need to be made aware of how the socio-political and legislative processes work, and to have their confidence raised that they need not be the helpless victims either of an evil status quo or of revolutionary destruction, but can be active as society's salt and light in the fight to protect, re-establish or introduce Christian ethical values. This kind of consciousness-raising is particularly important for those church members who are community leaders, opinion formers and decision makers — for example, parents, teachers, journalists and politicians. In a democracy (in which government depends on the consent of the governed), legislation depends on public opinion. Our Christian responsibility is to get into the public debate about current issues, boldly affirm, practice and argue what the Bible teaches, and so seek to influence public opinion for Christ.

How, then, shall we handle controversial topics? Many voices during the Consultation have urged us to be cautious. Modern problems of personal and social ethics (which are often inter-related) are legion: abortion, euthanasia, genetic engineering, homosexuality, racism, castism and tribalism, sexism, human rights, environmental pollution, ideologies, polygamy, economic inequality between and within nations, terrorism, war, nuclear disarmament, and many more. To some of these ethical questions the biblical answer is clear, and in most others a plain biblical principle is involved: here, then, the teaching of the church should be unequivocal and unanimous.

Yet, highly complex issues remain. So then, whenever the

Word of God speaks clearly, the church must speak clearly also, as for example did the German Confessing Church in the Barmen Declaration of 1934, and the Norwegian Church while Norway was under German occupation in World War II. If such speech is condemned as political, we need to remember that silence would be political, too. We cannot avoid taking sides. But when the teaching of Scripture seems unclear, and human reason has to seek to develop a position out of biblical principles, then the church should make a pronouncement only after thorough study and consultation.

When the church cannot agree on an issue, then the issue cannot be dealt with in the name of the church; instead, Christian individuals and groups should handle it. The church should also be sensitive to anything (such as a divisive controversy) that would weaken its evangelistic outreach. But when the church concludes that biblical faith or righteousness requires it to take a public stand on some issue, then it must obey God's Word and trust him with the consequences.

We heard from the pastor of a black church in New England that their resolve to address themselves to social issues has greatly increased their evangelistic witness. Their procedure is one of thorough consultation, in order to ensure unity rather than division in the congregation. First, the pastor makes a presentation on some issue to his deacons, next the deacons take it to the church council, and then the church council refers it to the church members. At each successive stage, agreement is sought. The result has been that the church has had wider opportunities for witness, because it has become known as a socially concerned church, and so evangelism and social action have had a multiplying impact on one another.

All of us are agreed that a local church should not normally engage in partisan politics, either advocating a particular party or attempting to frame political programmes. We also are agreed, however, that the local church has a prophetic ministry to proclaim the law of God and to teach justice, should seek to be the conscience of the community, and has a duty to help the congregation develop a Christian mind, so that the people may learn to think Christianly even about controversial questions.

4. Power

All of us agree that God gives power to his people — power for holiness, power for witness, and power for courageous action in the name of Christ. We all also agree that, in his sovereignty and his grace, God endows his people with a wide variety of spiritual gifts for service. Some of us lay particular emphasis on supernatural "gifts of healing", "the working of miracles" (I Cor. 12:9,10), and the casting out of demons, while others prefer to emphasize non-miraculous social gifts like contributing to the needs of others, giving aid, and doing "acts of mercy" (Rom. 12:8). All spiritual gifts, whatever their nature, should be exercised with compassion under the anointing of the Holy Spirit and for the common good. They can meet social, physical and emotional as well as spiritual needs, contribute to the well-being of society as well as of the church, and, authenticating the Gospel, draw unbelievers to Christ.

5. Vocations

All Christians are called to both witness and service. Whenever the opportunity is given, we have a privileged duty to speak for Christ and to serve our neighbour. In addition to this general Christian calling, however, each of us has a special vocation. We have already written about the diversity of gifts, leading to a diversity of ministries, in the Body of Christ.

The local church (especially its leadership) has a responsibility, therefore, to help its members (especially its young people) to recognize their gifts and so discover their vocation. Some churches set up a "vocation group" for those of its members who are wanting to discern God's will for their lives, in order that they may pray together, seek advice and investigate a variety of possibilities.

On the one hand, the local church should continuously keep before its membership the possibility that God may be calling some of them to a full-time Christian ministry as cross-cultural missionaries, evangelists, pastors, teachers, or church workers of some other kind. And the local church should give its members opportunities to test their vocation in evangelistic missions, house-to-house visitation, youth outreach, Sunday school teaching, and in other ways.

On the other hand, full-time Christian ministry is not limited to these areas. Although it is a great and sacred calling to be a missionary or a pastor, we must not thereby imply that other callings are "secular". There is an urgent need to encourage more of our Christian young people to respond to God's call into the professions, into industry and commerce, into public office in the political arena, and into the mass media, in order that they may penetrate these strongholds of influence for Christ. And whatever our church members' vocations are, we need both to help train them to serve there as Christians and to support them in their service.

This brings us back to evangelism again. For in order to make an impact on our society for Christ, we need more Christians to permeate it as his salt and light; otherwise, our effectiveness will be very small. But in order to send more Christians into the world, we must win more people for Christ and disciple them. "Our dire need," one of our groups has written, "is for an army of Josephs, Esthers, Daniels and Nehemiahs, who will have a determining voice in the affairs of our countries."

6. *Groups*

Just as there are special vocations, so there should be specialist groups in every church. For it is certain that the local church as a unit cannot possibly engage in all the activities it is being urged to undertake. Therefore, it must delegate particular responsibilities to different groups.

To begin with, there should be evangelistic groups, all trained for evangelistic outreach, one perhaps maintaining regular door-to-door visitation in the district, another organizing and maintaining a Christian coffee-bar or infiltrating a non-Christian one, another serving as a music group or witness team, another arranging evangelistic home meetings or home Bible study and prayer meetings. As the church responds sensitively to the evangelistic needs which it perceives in its community, appropriate new groups can constantly be brought into being.

In addition, the church needs social service groups. One may organize literacy classes with an ethnic minority, another may visit senior citizens or hospital patients or prison inmates, another may initiate a development project in a local slum area, or found a co-operative with the poor, or a club with delinquent youth, while another may offer citizens' advice or legal aid to those who cannot afford to pay for it. Again, the possibilities are almost limitless.

Thirdly, the local church may decide to form one or more social action groups, if this is compatible with its understanding of the church's role in society. Such groups would doubtless devote a good deal of their time to study, in which they may seek the help of experts. They might take up a global problem, in order to educate themselves and (if given the opportunity) the church. Or they might address themselves to an ethical issue like abortion. If they reach a consensus and are able to carry the church with them, then no doubt their study would lead to action, whether in terms of political lobbying or non-violent protest or joining in some national demonstration. An alternative to church groups is the encouragement of church members to join non-church groups.

Whatever action a group takes, however, it would have to be clear itself and make clear to others whether it is operating on its own or has the backing of the church. All these groups — for evangelism, social service or social action — need to relate closely to the church, reporting back regularly and seeking advice and support. In this way the ministry of the church can be greatly diversified.

7. *Resources*

The evangelistic and social work of the church depends on money as well as people. How much of its income each local church decides to allocate to evangelism, and how much to social responsibility, will depend on its particular circumstances. This will have to be settled by prayerful consultation and not by a simple formula, and it will be related to what other churches, government and voluntary agencies are doing.

Each local church needs to remember, however, that it is a manifestation in its own community of the universal church of Christ. Therefore, it has an international as well as a local responsibility. The world-wide Christian community should seek to develop a true "partnership . . . in giving and receiving" (Phil. 4:15). That is, gifts should flow in both directions, so that every giver is also a receiver, and every receiver a giver. For example, one church might send financial help to another, and in return receive a visit from an evangelist or Bible teacher of the other church. Such reciprocal Christian ministry can be extremely enriching, and should be fostered by mutual discussion of needs and resources.

The context for Christian thinking about resources should be the forecast that by the year A.D. 2000 the world's population is likely to exceed six billion people. This will dramatically increase the numbers of both unevangelized and needy people. Meanwhile, a comparatively small number of Westerners who live around the North Atlantic, together with some wealthy minorities elsewhere, continue to consume a disproportionate percentage of Planet Earth's natural wealth.

If Christians are going to take seriously the double challenge to take the Good News to all nations and to enable the poor to become self-reliant, a major redistribution of resources will be necessary. We are not now pronouncing on the controversial macro-question of how to redress the economic imbalance between rich and poor nations. Rather are we wanting wealthy local churches to remember that millions of poor people in the world are their Christian brothers and sisters. The Christian conscience cannot come to terms with the fact that they live and die in poverty, while so many of us enjoy an affluent life-style.

We are still committed to Paragraph 9 of the Lausanne Covenant, which commented that we cannot attain our goals without sacrifice, and then went on: "All of us are shocked by the poverty of millions and disturbed by the injustices which cause it. Those of us who live in affluent circumstances accept our duty to develop a simple life-style in order to contribute more generously to both relief and evangelism." We are not naive enough to imagine that the world's problems will be solved by such action. But we believe that a Christian life-style of contentment and simplicity fulfils the teaching of Scripture, expresses solidarity with the poor, and releases funds for evangelistic and social enterprises.

At present, only a tiny fraction of our total Christian resources is being applied to any kind of mission, evangelistic or social. How, then, can Christian people be motivated to give? The strongest argument for sacrificial giving is the one Paul used when appealing to the Christians of Corinth to be generous: "For you know the grace of our Lord Jesus Christ, that though he was rich, yet for your sake he became poor, so that by his poverty you might become rich" (II Cor. 8:9). Our Lord is generous; his people therefore must be generous, too. And the place to learn generosity is the local church.

(d) The Church under Repression

There are many settings in the world where today's church, like the early church, suffers from harassment or active persecution. We have thought particularly about churches repressed by Marxist, Muslim or extreme rightist regimes, and about minority churches repressed by state-related churches. In such situations, it has been suggested to us, the church always has faced three temptations — to *conform* (tailoring the Gospel to the prevailing ideology), to *fight* (losing its identity by resorting to worldly weapons), or to *withdraw* (denying its mission, betraying its calling, and losing its relevance). It also has been pointed out to us that there were three similar options in our Lord's day, represented by the Sadducees (the compromisers), the Zealots (the freedom fighters), and the Pharisees and Essenes (the escapists), and that these three groups formed an unholy alliance against Jesus, finding him a greater threat than each other.

Our brothers and sisters in repressive situations have recommended that, resisting these three temptations, the church should rather develop a critical involvement in society, while preserving its primary allegiance to Christ. Such a church will have little opportunity to preach openly or to exert a social influence, because it has been pushed to the margins of society and has no apparatus of power. The following guidelines for its evangelism and social responsibility have been proposed:

1. Consistency

Above all, the church must be true to its Lord, a Christ-centred community, and thus establish the credibility of its witness. There must be no dichotomy between its profession and its practice. For being precedes acting, and seeing must accompany hearing.

2. Love

Churches under duress should remember the evangelizing power of a Christian community of love which, even when public worship and witness are forbidden, can bear its testimony by deeds of love. Each local church needs to be a model of just structures, harmonious relationships, and modest lifestyle. The people of God need also to remember that their "enemies", who persecute them, are persons in whom is the image of God and for whom Christ died, and that a person is more important than the ideology which he or she holds. By the grace of God, they will be enabled to love their enemies, as Jesus taught.

3. Witness

Even under persecution, God opens spaces for his people to live and share the Gospel, especially in personal evangelism, and to demonstrate that the "new man" of Marxist expectation can be created only by Jesus Christ. God will give opportunities also to serve human need. Even though centrally-planned economies in some countries have succeeded in abolishing extreme poverty, there still remain pockets of deep human need — the disillusioned, the elderly, the lonely, and the neglected minority groups. Christians will gladly love and serve them.

4. Solidarity

When the church has to act, especially in some kind of protest, who will take the initiative? It is too risky for pastors, and individuals are too weak. So members of the Body of Christ must stand together, the local curch for local issues, and the national church for national issues, knowing their legal rights and defending them (like the apostle Paul), and witnessing together to Christ.

5. *Suffering*

What if church and state appear to be on a collision course?

The general teaching of Scripture is plain. The institution of government has been established by God; and citizens are required to be subject to it — to obey the law, pay their taxes, fulfil their civic duties, and seek the good of their country. Indeed, Christian people should encourage the state to perform its Godgiven duty to reward those who do right and punish those who do wrong (Rom. 13:1-7; I Pet. 2:13-15; cf. Jer. 29:7).

What happens if the state abuses its authority, however, and either forbids what God commands or commands what God forbids? The principle is clear. We are to obey the state (whose authority comes from God) right up to the point where obedience to it would involve us in disobedience to him. In that extreme circumstance alone, it is our Christian duty to disobey the state in order to obey God.

This has an evangelistic implication. It was when the Sanhedrin forbade the apostles to preach in the name of Jesus that Peter said, "We must obey God rather than men", and "We cannot but speak of what we have seen and heard" (Acts 4:17-20; 5:27-29). Those of us who live in free countries are in no position to tell our brothers and sisters in totalitarian situations how they should respond to government attempts to silence them. We do not think they necessarily should defy the authorities with the outspoken boldness of the apostles. They may consider it wiser at least in many cases to bear testimony more by deed than by word. On the other hand, they will be unable to give the state complete allegiance in this matter, since witness to Jesus is an inalienable part of our obedience to him.

Turning to social action, the Bible records a noble succession of men and women who risked their lives by courageously defying a human authority in the name of the God of justice. We have been reminded of Nathan, who confronted King David over his adultery with Bathsheba and his murder of her husband; of Elijah, who denounced King Ahab for annexing Naboth's vineyard by having him assassinated; of Daniel and his friends, who between them refused either to worship an image or to stop worshipping the true God; of Queen Esther, who dared to present herself, though unbidden, to King Ahasuerus in order to plead for her people unjustly condemned to be massacred; and of John the Baptist, who told King Herod that his marriage to Herodias his sister-in-law was unlawful, and who lost his life as a result.

With these biblical precedents we should not be surprised that they have their modern counterparts. Three African examples have particularly impressed us. When the President of Chad, in the name of cultural revolution, tried to force Christians to submit to pagan initiation rites, some compromised, others were killed, and the church leaders were unable to act in unison. A single layman, however, wrote an Open Letter to the President to explain why he could not submit, even if it meant that he must die. His letter was received and respected.

Although Kenya does not fall into the category of a repressive dictatorship, and Christians (who are in the majority) enjoy freedom, yet the church has on occasions suffered and has taken a firm stand against injustices. In 1969, some Kikuyu leaders tried to unite their tribe by requiring an oath of loyalty to it. Many Christians refused to take the oath because, they said, their supreme loyalty was to Christ, and their next loyalty was to their nation, not their tribe. Some were killed. So a group of church leaders went together to President Kenyatta, and as a result the oathing was stopped.

That confrontation with a President was successful. Another, in the neighbouring country of Uganda, led to tragedy, although God turned it to the church's good. During Amin's reign of terror, the House of Bishops of the Anglican Church of Uganda wrote him a joint letter to complain of the cruelty and malpractices of his soldiers, and of the total disregard for human life in the country. Archbishop Janani Luwum was summoned to appear before an assembly of leaders and soldiers, and then was falsely accused, mocked, and shortly afterwards assassinated. The other bishops stood in solidarity with him at this time of suffering.

These examples of courage have greatly challenged us. We believe that such confrontations should be reserved for extreme situations only and that in such circumstances church leaders, if possible, should act together and only after the most thorough consultation.

Nevertheless, there are occasions of moral principle in which the church must take its stand, whatever the cost. For the church is the community of the Suffering Servant who is also the Lord, and it is called to serve and suffer with him. It is not popularity which is the authentic mark of the church, but prophetic suffering, and even martyrdom. "Indeed all who desire to live a godly life in Christ Jesus will be persecuted" (II Tim. 3:14). May we be given grace to stand firm!

Conclusion: A Call to Obedience

We have come to the end of our report. It has been a great joy for us to be together for this week. Despite our different backgrounds and traditions, we have deeply appreciated one another and the rich multicultural fellowship which God has given us.

We have talked, listened, pondered, debated and prayed. We also have warned one another of the dangers of such prolonged analysis, categorization and reflection, while outside — beyond the delightful campus of the Reformed Bible College where we have been accommodated so comfortably — are living those lost, oppressed and needy people about whom we have been speaking.

Now the time has come for us to stop discussing them and start serving them, to leave "the mountain of glory" and descend to "the valley of problems and opportunities" (about which Bishop David Gitari preached during our opening service of worship).

Jesus our Lord is calling us to put into practice what we have written, and to determine afresh by his grace to reach all peoples with the Gospel. Challenged by the humility of his Incarnation, inspired by the love of his Cross, relying on the power of his Resurrection, and eagerly awaiting the glory of his Return, we are resolved to obey his call. We hope that others who read our report will be moved by the same Lord to the same resolve and the same obedience.

We request the Lausanne Committee for World Evangelization and the World Evangelical Fellowship, who jointly sponsored our Consultation, and other bodies of like mind, to call Christians and churches around the world to a more costly commitment to the lost, the needy and the oppressed, for the greater glory of God, Father, Son and Holy Spirit.

Grand Rapids, Michigan
26 June 1982

Appendix A

Members of the Consultation

'Members' is an inclusive term referring to several groups of persons involved in CRESR 82: ex officio *individuals, participants invited on a regional basis, and consultants from various fields of expertise. In this list they are placed in alphabetical order irrespective of the category to which each belonged.*

Tokunboh Adeyemo, Nigeria/Kenya
Sarah F. Anders, USA
Pedro Arana-Quiroz, Peru
Gonzalo Baez-Camargo, Mexico
Peter Beyerhaus, West Germany
Klaus Bockmuehl, Canada
David J. Bosch, South Africa
Hector Camacho, USA
Robinson Cavalcanti, Brazil
John C. Cho, South Korea
Wilson W. Chow, Hong Kong
Wade Coggins, USA
Harvie M. Conn, USA
Edward R. Dayton, USA
Eva Den Hartog, Holland/USA
Mariano di Gangi, Canada
Carmen Canelo Donoso, Chile
Leighton Ford, USA
David M. Gitari, Kenya
Samuel Habib, Egypt
Michael Haynes, USA
Arthur P. Johnston, USA
Peter Kuzmic, Yugoslavia
Harold Lindsell, USA
Robert Matzken, Netherlands
Lois McKinney, USA
Gordon Moyes, Australia
Ludwig Munthe, Norway
Abel Ndjerareou, Chad
Bruce Nicholls, N.Z./India
Agne Nordlander, Sweden
Emilio A. D. Nunez, Guatemala
Samuel A. Olson, Venezuela
Gottfried Osei-Mensah, Ghana/Kenya
C. René Padilla, Argentina
John Perkins, USA
Soeti Rahayoe, Indonesia
John R. Reid, Australia
D. John Richard, India
Bong Rin Ro, Taiwan
Vinay K. Samuel, India
Kefa Sempangi, Uganda
Ronald J. Sider, USA
Tom Sine, USA
John Stott, Great Britain
Christopher Sugden, G.B./India
Tite Tienou, Upper Volta
Dick L. Van Halsema, USA
Agustin B. Vencer, Philippines
C. Peter Wagner, USA
David F. Wells, USA

Appendix B

The Papers and their Writers

Day One: Church History and Modern Theologies

1. The Perspective of Church History — Bong Rin Ro
   Response: David Wells
2. Perspectives on Evangelism and Social Responsibility in Contemporary Theology (1954 to present) — Tokunboh Adeyemo
   Response: David Bosch

Day Two: Salvation and Kingdom

3. How Broad is Salvation in Scripture? — Ronald Sider
   Response: Ludwig Munthe
4. The Kingdom in Relation to the Church and the World — Arthur P. Johnston
   Response: René Padilla

Day Three: History and Eschatology

5. Evangelical Views — Peter Kuzmic
   Response: Emilio Antonio Nunez
6. A Biblical Encounter with Some Contemporary Non-Christian or Un-Evangelical Views — Peter Beyerhaus
   Response: Gordon Moyes

Day Four: The Mission of the Church

7. The Mission of the Church in Relation to Evangelism and Social Responsibility. A Biblical Study — Vinay Samuel and Chris Sugden
   Response: Harold Lindsell
8. A second presentation — John Chongnalm Cho
   Response: Tite Tienou